BUG BOOKS

Spider

Revised and Updated

Karen Hartley, Chris Macro, and Philip Taylor

Heinemann
LIBRARY

www.heinemann.co.uk/library

Visit our website to find out more information about Heinemann Library books.

To order:

☎ Phone 44 (0) 1865 888066

🖹 Send a fax to 44 (0) 1865 314091

💻 Visit the Heinemann Bookshop at www.heinemann.co.uk/library to browse our catalogue and order online.

First published in Great Britain by Heinemann Library, Halley Court, Jordan Hill, Oxford OX2 8EJ, part of Harcourt Education.
Heinemann is a registered trademark of Harcourt Education Ltd.

Editorial: Diyan Leake and Catherine Clarke
Design: Kimberly R. Miracle and Cavedweller Studio
Illustrations: Alan Fraser at Pennant Illustration
Picture research: Melissa Allison
Production: Alison Parsons

Originated by Dot Gradations Ltd
Printed and bound in China by South China Printing Company

ISBN 978 0 431 01981 9 (hardback)
12 11 10 09 08
10 9 8 7 6 5 4 3 2 1

ISBN 978 0 431 01987 1 (paperback)
12 11 10 09 08
10 9 8 7 6 5 4 3 2 1

British Library Cataloguing in Publication Data
Hartley, Karen, Macro, Chris and Taylor, Philip
Spider. - 2nd Edition.- (Bug Books)
595.7'26
A full catalogue record for this book is available from the British Library.

Acknowledgements
The publishers would like to thank the following for permission to reproduce photographs:
© Ardea pp. **4** (B. Gibbons), **7** (A. Warren), **9** (A. Warren), **11** (J. Clegg), **13** (B. Gibbons), **20** (B. Gibbons), **29** (T. Bomford); © Bruce Coleman pp. **5** (J. Burton), **6** (Dr F. Sauer), **14** (Dr F. Sauer), **15** (J. Jurka), **28** (A. Stillwell); © Garden and Wildlife Matters (M. Collins) p. **19**; © NaturePL (Bernard Castelein) p. **17**; © NHPA (S. Dalton) p. **22**; © Okapia (H. Reinhard) p. **24**; © Oxford Scientific Films pp. **8** (N. Bromhall), **10** (M. Black), **12** (S. Morris), **18** (M. Fogden), **21** (J. Cooke), **23** (M. Fogden), **25** (K. Atkinson), **26** (M. Leach); © Photolibrary (James Robinson) p. **16**; © Science Photo Library (Claude Nuridsany & Marie Perennou) p. **27**.

Cover photograph of a Chilean rose tarantula reproduced with permission of Getty Images (Tim Flach).

Every effort has been made to contact copyright holders of any material reproduced in this book. Any omissions will be rectified in subsequent printings if notice is given to the publishers.

Contents

Some words are shown in bold, **like this**. You can find out what they mean by looking in the glossary.

What are spiders?

leg

Spiders are small animals with eight legs. They are soft animals. They have no bones. Spiders cannot fly.

Most spiders make **webs**. They make silk inside their bodies and then build a web out of it. **Insects** get stuck in the sticky web. Then the spiders eat them.

5

What do spiders look like?

eye

fang

Most spiders have eight eyes. They also have two **fangs**. They use their fangs to poison **insects**.

Spiders are usually brown or grey. Some can change colour so they cannot be seen by enemies. This crab spider has turned yellow like the flower it is sitting on.

How big are spiders?

Male spiders are smaller than **female** spiders. Some spiders are smaller than the full stop at the end of this line.

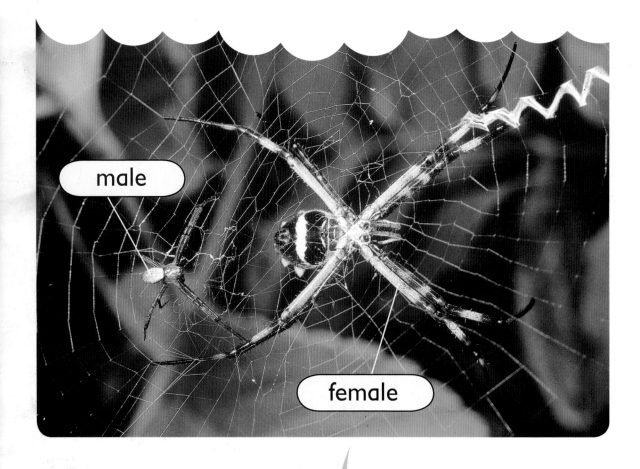

male

female

Spiders that live in hot countries can grow bigger than your hand. Some spiders are so big they can eat birds and frogs.

How are spiders born?

The **male** spider taps on the **female's web**. This tells the female that he is not an **insect**. They **mate** and the female spider lays eggs.

10

cocoon

Female spiders make a bag of silk to lay their eggs in. This bag is called a **cocoon**. The spider puts the cocoon in a safe place. The baby spiders usually **hatch** out after a few days.

11

How do spiders grow?

new skin

old skin

When baby spiders grow, they make a new skin. The old skin drops off. This is called **moulting**. Most spiders do this up to nine times before they are fully grown.

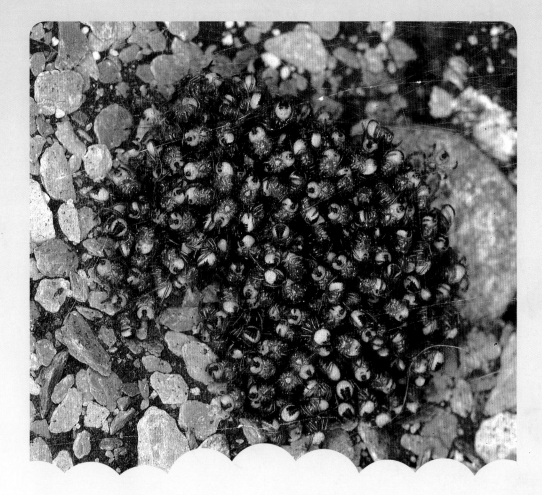

Baby spiders look like their parents,
but they are very tiny. Young spiders
are called spiderlings.

How do spiders move?

Spiders use their eight legs to walk or run. They move their legs two at a time. Some spiders can move as fast as humans.

Crab spiders can walk sideways and backwards. Spiders have special pads on their feet. This stops them from sticking to their **webs**.

web

What do spiders eat?

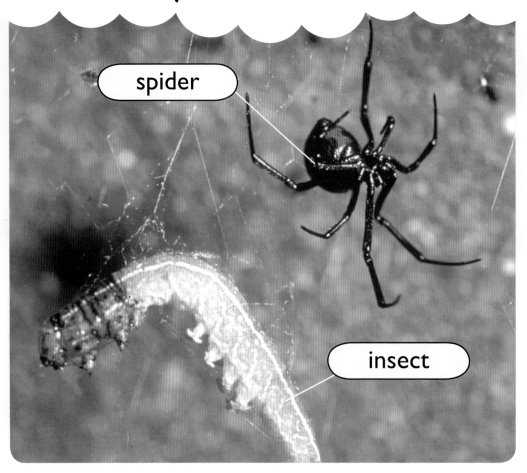

spider

insect

Spiders eat flies and other **insects**. The insects get stuck in the **web**. Spiders poison the insects with their **fangs**. The poison makes the inside of the insects soft.

spider

insect

Spiders suck the soft parts of the insect up into their mouths. They leave the hard outside part. Some very big spiders eat lizards, birds, and frogs.

Which animals eat spiders?

hunting wasp

spider

Hunting wasps jump on spiders. They carry them back to a tunnel in the ground. The spiders cannot move. The wasp's larvae eat the spider alive.

Birds, snakes, ants, and frogs also like to eat spiders. Spiders are even eaten by other spiders.

Where do spiders live?

You can find spiders in parks, woodlands, gardens, and even in your house. Some live in holes between stones. Some live under leaves where it is damp.

Some tiny spiders live in the fur of big animals. In hot countries, some spiders live in holes in the ground. Many spiders live in dark caves.

How long do spiders live?

Many spiders die when they are babies.
Most **adult** spiders live for about a year.
Sometimes the **female** spider eats the
male spider after they have **mated**.

tarantula

A tarantula is a big spider that lives in hot countries. Some people like to keep tarantulas as pets. They can live for 20 years as pets.

What do spiders do?

Spiders make **webs** and look for food.
Most spiders build their webs early in the
morning. This takes about an hour. Spiders
rest in quiet dark places.

The funnelweb spider lives under the ground. It makes a **burrow** where it can stay cool and damp. Then it spins silk to make the burrow soft.

spider

How are spiders special?

Spiders have special hairs on their legs. The hairs move if an **insect** lands on the **web**. This tells the spider that food is coming.

hair

leg

Spiders are special because they can make strong silk. The silk comes out of **spinnerets**. The spinnerets are like little fingers underneath the spider.

spinneret

Thinking about spiders

This spider is hiding on a flower. It has changed its colour so it cannot be seen very well. Why do you think the spider would need to hide like this? What do you think this spider eats?

How long do you think it has taken the spider to make this **web**? How does the web help the spider?

29

Bug map

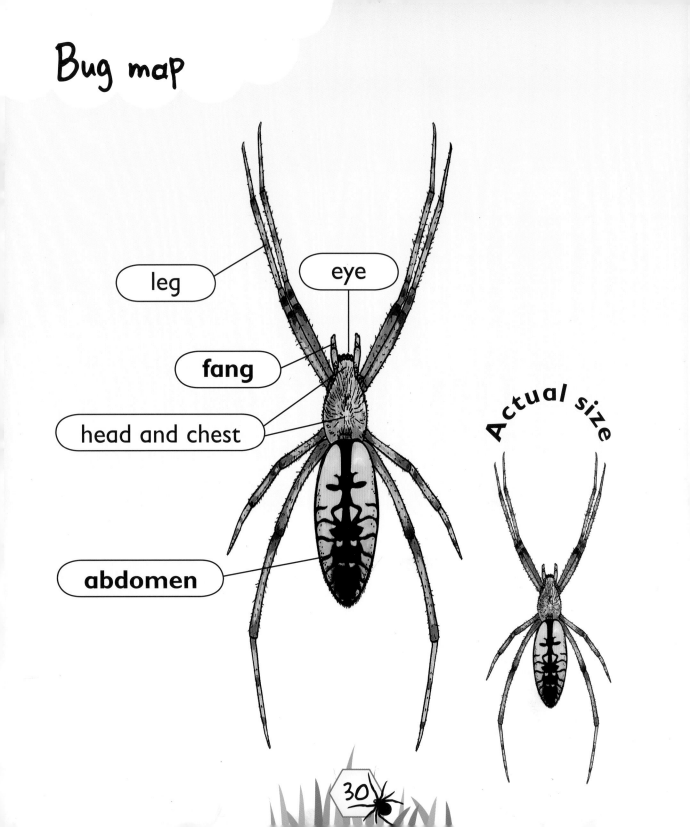

leg

eye

fang

head and chest

abdomen

Actual size

Glossary

abdomen stomach area

adult grown-up

burrow long hole that looks like a tunnel in the ground

cocoon silk bag that a female spider makes to hold her eggs

fang claw on a spider's head. It is used to poison insects.

female animal that can lay eggs or give birth to young. Women are females.

hatch break out of an egg

insect small animal with six legs and a body with three parts

male animal that can mate with a female to produce young. Men are males.

mate when a male and female come together to make babies

moulting time in an insect's life when it gets too big for its skin. The old skin drops off and a new skin is underneath.

spinneret part of a spider's body that is used for making silk

web net made from sticky threads of silk. Spiders use webs to catch food.

Index

More books to read

My First Book of Bugs and Spiders, Dee Phillips (Tick Tock Media, 2005)

Spiders Up Close, Greg Pyres (Raintree, 2005)

Watch it Grow: Spider, Barrie Watts (Franklin Watts, 2004)